THE Allergy-Free Vegan

Monica Levin
www.MonicaLevin.com   www.JoinMonica.com

The information presented in this book is based on the training and experience of the author, Monica Levin. It is not intended to diagnose illness or prescribe treatment. Rather this material is designed to be the reader's companion on their journey of self-discovery and health. This book contains a portion on the information which is available on Monica's website www.JoinMonica.com.

The Allergy-Free Vegan

Copyright © 2010 Monica Levin

Published by Lulu.com

ISBN: 978-0-557-45081-7

This book is dedicated to YOU!

1 Food Allergy 2 Gluten-Free 3 Wheat-Free
4 Lactose-Free 5 Corn-Free 6 Recipes 7 Desserts
8 Vegan 9 Vegetarian

TABLE OF CONTENTS

INTRODUCTION 7
NAVIGATING THE COOKBOOK 8
EXTRAS 10
   Almond Mayonnaise 11
   Apple Tea 12
   Avocado Almond Dip 13
   Banana Shake 14
   Bean Spread 15
   Cannelli Bean Dip 16
   Flaxseed "Goop" 17
   Cilantro Sauce 18
   Cracker Spread 19
   Date Spread 20
   Date Coconut Spread 21
   Fruit Spread 22
   Nut Milk 23
   Mango Chutney 24
   Pesto I 25
   Pesto II 26
   Plantain 27
   Sesame Seasoning 28
   Split Pea Spread 29
   Sun-Dried Tomato Spread 30
   Tofu Mayonnaise 31
VEGETABLES 32
   Baked Yams 33
   Basil Tomato Sauce 34
   Bean-Stuffed Squash 35
   Beets and Ginger 36
   Beets and Carrots 37
   Broccoli Carrot Medley 38
   Broccoli Soup 39
   Broiled Vegetable Kabobs 40
   Cauliflower with Black Beans 41
   Cooked Vegetable Idea 42
   Curried Pear and Parsnip Soup 43
   Eggplant Dip #1 44
   Eggplant Dip #2 45
   Eggplant Slices with Roma Tomatoes 46
   Green Beans with Hazelnuts 47
   Herbed Spinach 48

Italian-Style Greens 49
Parsley Mushrooms 50
Roasted Fennel and Onions 51
Roasted Red Pepper and Navy Bean Salad 52
Roasted Vegetables #1 53
Roasted Vegetables #2 54
Roasted Vegetables #3 55
Scalloped Yams and Apples 56
Sesame Vegetables 57
Spiced Pumpkin Soup 58
Tomato Zucchini Sauce 59
Zucchini with Raisins and Pine Nuts 60

SALADS 61
Avocado Dressing 62
Dijon Mustard Dressing 63
French Dressing 64
Ginger-Sesame Dressing 65
Lime Vinaigrette 66
Sesame Salad Dressing 67
Tofu Sesame Dressing 68
Avocado Salad 69
Bean Sprout Salad 70
Carrot Celery Salad 71
Cooked Vegetable Salad 72
Green Bean Salad 73
Kale Salad 74
Marinated Salad 75
Spinach Salad 76
Tabouli 77
Waldorf Salad 78
Watercress and Radicchio Salad 79

STARCHES 80
Basic Millet 81
Basic Quinoa 82
Basic Rice 83
Brown Rice Chili 84
Buckwheat Pilaf 85
Curried Oat Groats 86
Curried Rice Salad 87
Garlic Rosemary Potatoes 88
Garlic Walnut Brown Rice 89
Hash Brown Potatoes 90
High Protein Oatmeal 91
Indian Flat Bread 92

- Mediterranean Pasta Salad 94
- Millet Polenta 95
- Millet and Squash 96
- Pesto Pasta Salad 97
- Quinoa Stir Fry 98
- Rice Stir Fry 99
- Rice Vermicelli Salad 100
- Three Grain Salad 101

LEGUMES 102
- Azuki Bean Soup 103
- Bean Salad I 104
- Bean Salad II 105
- Chickpea Dip 106
- Chickpea and Spinach Soup 107
- Curried Chickpeas 108
- Falafel with Tahini Sauce 109
- Lima Beans Salad 110
- Lima Beans in Tomato Sauce 111
- Mixed Bean Soup 112
- Navy Beans Provençale 113
- Sesame Crusted Tofu 114
- Soy Yogurt 115
- Tofu Quiche 116
- Tuscan Kidney Beans With Sage 117
- Vegetable Chili 118

DESSERTS 119
- Amaranth Muffins 120
- Apple Flax Treat 121
- Apple Oat Dessert 122
- Arrowroot Pancakes 123
- Barley Pancakes 124
- Blueberry Crisp 125
- Brown Rice Pudding 126
- Buckwheat Currant Dessert 127
- Chocolate Pudding 128
- Cranberry Muffins 129
- Energy Balls 130
- Fruit in "Gelatin" 131
- Fruit Juice Muffins 132
- Granola 133
- Indian Fruit Bake 134
- Indian Pudding 135
- Nut-Apricot Cobbler 136

Nut-Carob Cookies 137
Nut Pancakes 138
Oatmeal and Fruit Pudding 139
Peach Crisp 140
Pear Crumble 141
Poached Peaches 142
Raisin Pudding 143
Raisin-Sauced Pears 144
Rice Flour Pancakes 145
Strawberries and Lemon 146
Tapioca Pudding I 147
Tapioca Pudding II 148

INTRODUCTION

Welcome to "The Allergy-Free Vegan". This cookbook is a compilation of recipes from clients and friends who have been following an allergy-free diet and have decided to avoid eating animal products. All of the recipes are made without:

- wheat and wheat products (including spelt and kamut)
- corn
- salt
- sweeteners (except from fruits)
- animal products

I have not tried all of the recipes so play with the quantities, cooking temperatures, and cooking times. Add the ingredients that you feel inspired to add and omit the ones you dislike. Some of the recipes are decidedly vague and invite your input more than others. Have fun with your meal preparation and remember that simple is often "better"!

Wishing you health and happiness, Monica

Note: All of the recipes in this book can also be found on my membership website www.JoinMonica.com.

NAVIGATING THE COOKBOOK

I was guided to put the recipes in several categories:

- ➢ extras
- ➢ vegetables
- ➢ salads
- ➢ starches
- ➢ legumes
- ➢ desserts

It seems, though, that many recipes could fall into more than one category! For example, the Roasted Red Pepper and Navy Bean Salad could be in the "vegetable" category, the "salad" category, or the "legume" category.

To help yourself navigate the cookbook put notes to yourself on the recipe pages indicating what you like to serve with that dish and what page number it is on for future reference. If the recipes come from another cookbook remember to include the title of that book in your notes.

Do not allow yourself to be influenced by the word "dessert". The recipes in this section can be used for breakfasts, snacks, or even lunch or dinner. Similarly the recipes in the "extras" category can be used to accompany any meal. For example Banana Shake could be followed by Date Coconut Spread on wheat-free bread or crackers for supper, or Pesto I on wheat-free noodles could be for breakfast! Use your imagination and allow yourself to be guided to what is best for you to eat in this moment, without judgment.

"The Allergy-Free Vegan" excludes recipes that contain animal products. This by no means implies that you must be vegan in order to use this cookbook. If you eat "flesh" foods serve lamb chops with Eggplant Slices with Roma Tomatoes or roast chicken with Roasted Vegetables #2 and Green Bean Salad. If you are someone who chooses to consume animal products try to reduce the frequency to once every three to four days and choose more easily digestible "flesh" like fish or eggs,

For those of you that try to eat a high protein diet concentrate on the recipes in the "legume" category and any recipes with quinoa or millet in the "starches" category. Reduce consuming dishes made with the other grains and dishes made with potatoes.

For those of you that try to eat mostly vegetables this book is ideal. The different spreads, the sauces, the pestos, and the chutney all make plain steamed vegetables more exciting.

Regardless of your diet goals this book is a great basic tool for better eating and better living. Remember you can choose to live to eat or you can choose to eat to live. May you live a healthy life full of joy and peace.

Best, Monica

EXTRAS

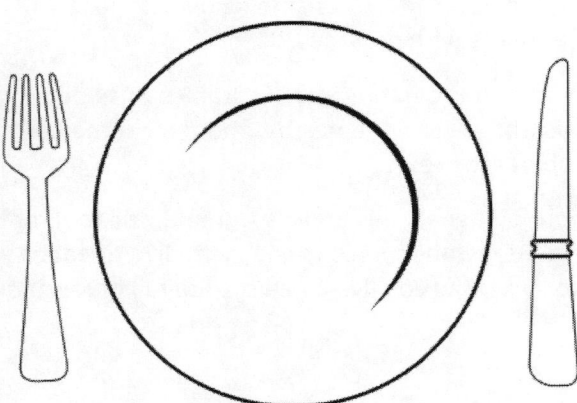

Almond Mayonnaise	11
Apple Tea	12
Avocado Almond Dip	13
Banana Shake	14
Bean Spread	15
Cannelli Bean Dip	16
Flaxseed "Goop"	17
Cilantro Sauce	18
Cracker Spread	19
Date Spread	20
Date Coconut Spread	21
Fruit Spread	22
Nut Milk	23
Mango Chutney	24
Pesto I	25
Pesto II	26
Plantain	27
Sesame Seasoning	28
Split Pea Spread	29
Sun-Dried Tomato Spread	30
Tofu Mayonnaise	31

Almond Mayonnaise

In a blender or food processor blend until a thick cream forms:

½ cup blanched almonds   **½ cup water**

Add and blend thoroughly:

1 small garlic sliver   **dash of cayenne pepper**

3 tbsp lemon juice   **black pepper to taste**

Drizzle in olive oil slowly, while beating continuously, until the mixture will no longer take in any more oil.

2 to 3 cups olive oil

Refrigerate in a glass jar.

Apple Tea

Place in a saucepan and bring to a boil:

8 ounces dried apple slices **4 whole cloves**

2 sticks cinnamon **5 cups water**

Reduce heat and simmer 15 minutes.

Strain into tea cups, pressing apple slices gently to remove all the liquid.

Note: Eat remaining apple slices with oatmeal sprinkled with chopped nuts.

Avocado Almond Dip

Blend together in a food processor until it has a smooth consistency:

- ¼ cup olive oil
- 1 stalk (or ½ cup) chopped celery
- ¼ cup almond butter
- 2 tbsp lemon juice
- 2 avocados, peeled and sliced

Banana Shake

In a blender mix:

    1 cup water   **1 tbsp all-fruit jam**

    2 frozen bananas   **1 tsp flaxseed oil**

Serve.

Variation: Add ½ cup frozen fruit such as raspberries, blueberries, or mangoes.

Bean Spread

Soak overnight:

1 cup Romano or pinto beans **5 cups water**

Drain and rise beans. Add additional water and cook until tender:

5 cups water

Drain the beans.

Add the following and process in a food processor until smooth:

1 tbsp olive oil **1 tsp ground cumin**

1 tsp dried basil **½ tsp ground black pepper**

Roll with alfalfa sprouts into lettuce leaves, or serve with rice crackers.

Variation: Add a dash of cayenne pepper.

Cannelli Bean Dip

Soak overnight:

    3/4 cup cannelli beans (white kidney beans)

    5 cups water

Drain and rinse beans. Add additional water and cook until tender:

    5 cups water

Drain the beans and set aside.

Process the following in a food processor until smooth:

    1 large tomato, coarsely chopped

    1 medium onion, coarsely chopped

    1 hot chili pepper, halved and seeded

2 cloves garlic	**4 tsp chili powder**
2 tbsp wheat-free soy sauce	**2 tsp ground cumin**

Add beans and process until smooth.

Variation: Use other white beans such as lima beans, navy beans, or great northern beans.

Flaxseed "Goop"

In a pot combine the following and bring to a boil:

1 cup water   **1/3 cup of ground flaxseeds**

Reduce heat and simmer for three minutes. Cool and transfer to a container and store in the fridge.

Use 2 tbsp of flaxseed "goop" as a substitute for each egg called for in your recipes.

Cilantro Sauce

Place the following ingredients in a food processor and process until all ingredients are thoroughly combined:

- ½ cup fresh parsley leaves
- 1 cup fresh cilantro (coriander) leaves
- 1 clove garlic, crushed
- 2 tbsp red wine vinegar
- 1 tbsp fresh lemon juice
- 3 tbsp olive oil
- freshly ground black pepper

Cracker Spread

In a food processor blend together:

1 pound pitted black olives   **¼ cup olive oil**

2 cloves garlic, crushed

Mix together and add to the processed mixture above:

2 tbsp Dijon mustard   **1 crushed bay leaf**

¼ tsp thyme   **1 clove garlic, crushed**

Serve with rice crackers.

Date Spread

Soak until dates are soft:

2 ½ cups chopped dates   **1 ½ cups hot water**

Add:

2 tsp organic lemon rind

Process in a blender until smooth.

Note: To make smoother cook over low heat, stirring constantly and adding more water if necessary.

Variation: Add 1 cup finely chopped hazelnuts.

Note: Use instead of date syrup in the Energy Balls.

Date Coconut Spread

Soak until dates are soft:

    7 to 9 dates　　　　　　　　**¾ cup hot water**

Add:

    2 tsp organic orange rind　　　**¼ cup almonds**

    2 tbsp dried unsweetened coconut

Process in a blender until smooth.

Note: Serve over cooked rice or as an accompaniment to a curry.

Fruit Spread

Combine the following a soak overnight:

½ cup dried apricots	½ cup currants
½ cup prunes	¼ cup almonds
1 ¼ cups apple juice	

Process in a blender, half at a time, to yield a purée.

Use on pancakes or with roasted vegetables.

Nut Milk

Put in a blender and blend at high speed for about 60 seconds:

4 cups water

¾ cup raw blanched almonds or raw cashews

Keep refrigerated.

Note: Shake well before using.

Mango Chutney

Peel and cut flesh into ½ inch cubes:

    2 medium mangoes

Add:

    2 tbsp finely chopped fresh cilantro (coriander)

    1 tbsp finely chopped fresh ginger root

    1/8 tsp ground hot red pepper

Mix gently to combine. Serve at once or cover tightly and refrigerate for no more than 8 hours before serving.

Pesto I

This is the more traditional of the two recipes for pesto and is made with basil.

In a blender or food processor blend until smooth:

2 cups tightly packed basil leaves

1 clove garlic, crushed   **½ cup olive oil**

2 tbsp pine nuts or walnuts   **¼ tsp ground black pepper**

Store, with a thin layer of olive oil on top, in a glass jar, in the refrigerator.

Note: Pesto can also be frozen. Spoon into ice cube trays, drizzle a layer of olive oil on top, and freeze.

Pesto II

This pesto recipe is a bit unusual in that it uses sun-dried tomatoes as its base.

Put in a saucepan:

3 ounces sun-dried tomatoes	**water to just cover**

Bring to a boil, reduce heat, and simmer for a couple of minutes. Remove from heat and let sit for one hour to rehydrate.

Drain the tomatoes, reserving the cooking water.

Place the rehydrated tomatoes in a food processor and add:

¼ cup pine nuts	**2 tbsp balsamic vinegar**
¼ cup walnuts	**2 tbsp cooking water**
¼ cup olive oil	**ground black pepper to taste**
½ cup chopped fresh basil leaves	**pinch of tarragon**

Process until smooth, adding a bit of the cooking water if it seems too thick.

Plantain

Plantains look like large green bananas. If you do not have any plantains around you can use bananas.

Peel and cut into ¼ inch slices:

1 plantain

Sauté until tender in:

3 to 4 tbsp olive oil

Serve immediately with a squeeze of:

lemon juice or lime juice

Note: The cooked plantains are sweet and are a great side dish with brown rice and oven-roasted vegetables.

Sesame Seasoning

Heat in a dry skillet until they begin to pop:

½ cup sesame seeds

Remove from heat and grind in a coffee grinder.

Add:

½ tsp ground black pepper   **½ tsp ground coriander**

Use this seasoning in place of salt at the table.

Split Pea Spread

In a food processor blend together:

> ¾ cup yellow split peas, rinsed, drained, and cooked

> 1/3 cup walnuts, chopped   2 green onions, chopped

> 1 clove garlic, crushed   3 tbsp lemon juice

> ¼ cup tofu   3 tbsp olive oil

Season with:

> freshly ground black pepper to taste

Transfer to a serving bowl and garnish with:

> walnut pieces   chopped green onions

Serve with wheat-free crackers or raw vegetables.

Sun-Dried Tomato Spread

Soak for an hour or two:

    ½ cup sun-dried tomatoes   **enough water to cover**

Drain the tomatoes and purée in a food processor with:

    3 cloves garlic, crushed   **¼ cup olive oil**

    3 tbsp black olive paste   **2 tbsp balsamic vinegar**

    1 green onion, minced   **ground black pepper to taste**

Use with crackers or on wheat-free bread with oven-roasted vegetables.

Note: This spread will last in the refrigerator for a couple of weeks.

Tofu Mayonnaise

In a food processor blend together:

1 cup firm tofu (6.5 ounces)   **2 tbsp chopped onion**

While continuing to blend, add:

¼ cup olive oil

Add and blend until smooth:

3 tbsp lemon juice

paprika, dill, mustard, or cayenne to taste

VEGETABLES

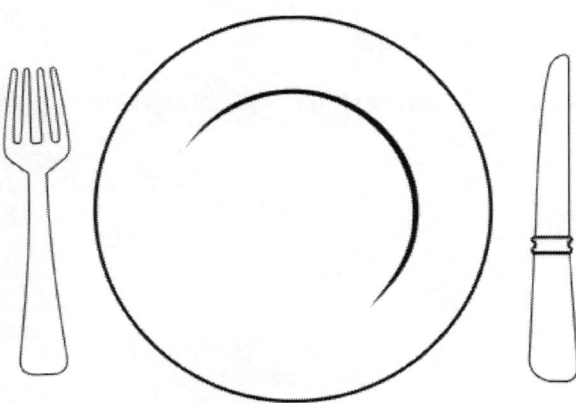

Basil Tomato Sauce 34
Bean-Stuffed Squash 35
Beets and Ginger 36
Beets and Carrots 37
Broccoli Carrot Medley 38
Broccoli Soup 39
Broiled Vegetable Kabobs 40
Cauliflower with Black Beans 41
Cooked Vegetable Idea 42
Curried Pear and Parsnip Soup 43
Eggplant Dip #1 44
Eggplant Dip #2 45
Eggplant Slices with Roma Tomatoes 46
Green Beans with Hazelnuts 47
Herbed Spinach 48
Italian-Style Greens 49
Parsley Mushrooms 50
Roasted Fennel and Onions 51
Roasted Red Pepper and Navy Bean Salad 52
Roasted Vegetables #1 53
Roasted Vegetables #2 54
Roasted Vegetables #3 55
Scalloped Yams and Apples 56
Sesame Vegetables 57
Spiced Pumpkin Soup 58
Tomato Zucchini Sauce 59
Zucchini with Raisins and Pine Nuts 60

Baked Yams

Preheat oven to 425°F.

Wash and scrub:

> **Yams (note: try to pick yams that are all similar in size)**

Bake 40 to 60 minutes, or until soft.

Variation: Use potatoes.

Variation: Wrap beets in aluminum foil and bake for 30 to 45 minutes, or until tender. Remove from oven. When cool enough to handle unwrap, slip off skins, and serve.

Basil Tomato Sauce

In a heavy saucepan sauté over medium heat until transparent but not brown:

    1 tbsp olive oil   **2 cloves garlic, crushed**

    ½ cup onion, diced

Reduce heat to minimum and add:

    one 28 ounce can tomato purée   **ground black pepper to taste**

    10 to 15 fresh basil leaves, chopped

Simmer for 30 to 40 minutes, or until flavors blend.

Use or freeze.

Bean-Stuffed Squash

Preheat oven to 350°F.

Cut in half, lengthwise and scoop out seeds:

> **3 acorn squash**

Place the halves, cut-side-down, in a shallow baking dish. Add:

> **one inch hot water**

Bake for 30 minutes.

Remove from the oven, drain off the water and turn the squashes so that they are cut-side-up.

Combine:

> **1 ½ cups cooked brown rice** **2 tbsp olive oil**
>
> **1 ½ cups cooked black beans** **1 tsp ground cinnamon**
>
> **1 ½ cups unsweetened applesauce** **¼ tsp ground cardamom**

Spoon into squash hollows and return to the oven.

Bake until squash is tender and the filling is heated through, about 30 minutes longer.

Beets and Ginger

Trim off greens and place in a saucepan with cold water and bring to a boil. Reduce heat and simmer until tender.

- **4 medium beets**

Drain and cover with cold water. Let stand until cool enough to handle. Peel and cut into slices.

Cut onion into thin wedges and sauté over medium-high heat until they brown:

- **1 medium onion**
- **1 tbsp grated ginger root**
- **2 tbsp olive oil**

Add beets and heat until warmed through.

Serve.

Beets and Carrots

Delicious served with "couscous".

Trim off greens and place in a saucepan with cold water and bring to a boil. Reduce heat and simmer until tender.

    8 small beets

Drain and cover with cold water. Let stand until cool enough to handle. Peel and cut into chunks or wedges.

Cut into chunks the same size as the beets then cook in water until just tender.

    8 carrots

Drain and rinse under cold water.

Soak for 15 minutes:

    ½ cup raisins   **¾ cup hot water**

Sauté beets and carrots for 2 to 3 minutes in:

    2 tbsp olive oil

Add and simmer for another 2 to 3 minutes:

    soaked raisins (including the liquid)   **1 tbsp lemon juice**

    1 tbsp grated lemon rind   **½ tsp ground cinnamon**

Add and cook until wilted:

    6 cups tightly packed beet greens, Swiss chard, or curly endive, which have been cut into thin strips

Stir in to season:

    3 tbsp chopped fresh mint   **¼ tsp ground black pepper**

Serve.

Broccoli Carrot Medley

Steam until just tender:

3 carrots, cut into ¼ inch rounds

Steam until just tender:

1 cup broccoli florets

In a bowl combine the carrots and broccoli and add:

one orange, peeled and cut into bite-sized pieces

Let stand for 15 to 30 minutes for flavors to blend.

Serve at room temperature.

Broccoli Soup

Blend in a food processor or blender until smooth:

    2/3 cup diced cucumber   **2 tbsp wheat-free soy sauce**

    ¾ cup water   **2 tsp olive oil**

    ¼ cup tahini

Add:

    4 to 5 cups broccoli florets

Blend. Transfer to a saucepan, warm, and then serve.

Broiled Vegetable Kabobs

Alternate any or all of the following vegetables onto soaked wooden skewers:

red, yellow, orange, or green pepper
   (cored, seeded, and cut into one inch square pieces)

yellow or green zucchini (cut into ½ inch rounds)

onion (peeled and cut into one inch square pieces)

button mushrooms

cherry tomatoes

Brush vegetable kabobs with olive oil and cook under your broiler in your oven (remember to keep the oven door partially or completely open such that the broiler functions properly).

Turn skewers as vegetables brown. Remove when cooked.

Serve warm or at room temperature with mango chutney, pesto, or cilantro sauce.

Cauliflower with Black Beans

In a large sauté pan heat together for 15 to 20 seconds:

- **2 tbsp olive oil**
- **½ tsp ground cumin**
- **1 tsp curry powder**
- **½ tsp ground coriander**

Add and cook until cauliflower is well-coated and nearly all of the liquid has evaporated, about 4 to 5 minutes:

- **1 small cauliflower, cored and cut into florets**
- **½ tsp crushed red pepper flakes**
- **¼ cup water**

Add the following, cover, and simmer until slightly thickened (about ten minutes):

- **one 14 ounce can of crushed tomatoes**
- **¼ cup water**

Gently stir in:

- **one 19 ounce can of black beans, rinsed and drained**

Cook until beans are heated through.

Sprinkle with:

- **2 tbsp finely chopped fresh cilantro**

Serve with Basic Millet and a salad of choice.

Cooked Vegetable Idea

You can do this with most cooked vegetables!

Steam or boil until just tender:

      any vegetable such as carrots, beet, green beans,

      wax beans, parsnips, potatoes, yams,

      turnip, zucchini, peppers, or asparagus

Allow to cool.

Serve at room temperature with Dijon mustard or with Dijon Mustard Dressing.

Curried Pear and Parsnip Soup

In a large pot cook the following ingredients together until the parsnips are soft:

- **4 ½ cups water**
- **4 ½ cups parsnips, chopped**
- **1 cup pears, peeled and chopped**
- **1 onion, chopped**
- **2 tsp curry powder**
- **1/4 tsp ground black pepper**
- **1 bay leaf**

Remove the bay leaf and purée the soup. Return to the pot, and reheat with:

- **1 cup rice milk**

Serve.

Eggplant Dip #1

Preheat oven to 350°F.

Cut off the stalk and bake for 30 to 40 minutes, or until soft all over and partially collapsed:

>**1 large or 2 small eggplants**

Cool and remove skin.

Blend in a food processor with the following ingredients until smooth:

>**1/3 cup lemon juice**   **6 tbsp tahini**
>
>**2 tbsp olive oil**   **1 clove garlic, crushed**
>
>**2 tbsp water**

Add more water if you like a thinner dip. Chill 2 to 3 hours or overnight.

Serve with raw vegetables or wheat-free crackers.

Eggplant Dip #2

Preheat oven to 400°F.

Cut off the stalk and bake for 30 to 40 minutes, or until soft all over and partially collapsed:

3 medium eggplants (about 3 to 4 pounds)

Cool and remove skin. Place in a bowl and mash with a fork until smooth. Chop the flesh coarsely.

Cook over low to medium heat until a deep golden brown:

3 medium onions   **3 to 4 tbsp olive oil**

Add:

½ cup red wine

Simmer, stirring often, for a minute or two. Season to taste with:

ground black pepper   **chopped fresh oregano**

Stir soft brown onions into the chopped eggplant. Stir in:

juice of one lemon

Serve warm or at room temperature with raw vegetables or wheat-free crackers.

Eggplant Slices with Roma Tomatoes

Preheat oven to 400°F.

Cut into half inch slices:

one large eggplant

Place slices directly on the oven racks for ten minutes (turning once after five minutes) to dry the eggplant.

Place slightly dried eggplant slices on a greased cookie sheet.

Mound the eggplant slices with:

8 Roma tomatoes, seeded and cut into small cubes

On each eggplant round put:

olive oil (2 tsp for each)   **freshly ground black pepper**

Reduce oven heat to 350°F and bake for 25 to 35 minutes.

Serve at room temperature with additional olive oil and toasted wheat-free bread or on wheat-free crackers.

Green Beans with Hazelnuts

Preheat oven to 350°F.

Bake for 5 minutes:

> **½ cup raw hazelnuts**

Remove, cool, and chop. Set aside.

Snip the ends off of:

> **2 pounds green beans**

Steam in a pot until barely tender. Drain and set aside.

Sauté in a large saucepan until shallots are barely tender:

> **3 tbsp olive oil**   **1 tsp chopped fresh rosemary**
> **¾ cup chopped shallots**

Add green beans and toss until heated through.

Add toasted hazelnuts and:

> **freshly ground black pepper to taste**

Serve.

Herbed Spinach

Wash and drain:

    1 ½ to 2 pounds spinach leaves

In a large pan sauté for one minute over medium-high heat:

2 tbsp olive oil	**1 tbsp chopped fresh tarragon**
2 tbsp chopped green onion	**2 tbsp chopped fresh thyme**
2 tbsp chopped chives	

Add spinach and sauté for 3 to 5 minutes, or until wilted.

Transfer to a serving dish and lightly toss with:

    3 tbsp lemon juice

Serve warm.

Italian-Style Greens

Wash and dry the following greens, then stack and cut crosswise into ribbons.

        2 pounds combination of dark green leafy vegetables

        such as Swiss chard, kale, mustard greens, endive,

        escarole, dandelion leaves, arugula, or rapini

In a large pan sauté over medium-high heat:

    2 tbsp olive oil   **1 clove garlic, finely chopped**

Add the greens and sauté for approximately 5 minutes, or until tender.

Serve.

Variation: Serve as an alternative to tomato sauce for your rice pasta dishes.

Parsley Mushrooms

Wash, pat dry, and cut into thin slices:

4 cups mushrooms (whichever kind you like)

Set mushrooms aside.

Wash, dry, and finely chop:

½ cup parsley

Set chopped parsley aside.

Over medium-high heat sauté until golden brown:

2 tbsp olive oil   **2 cloves garlic, sliced**

1 medium onion, cut into thin wedges   **1 tsp ground black pepper**

Add the mushrooms and continue to cook over medium-high heat until the mushrooms are golden brown.

Add the parsley and cook for an additional two minutes.

Serve.

Roasted Fennel and Onions

Preheat oven to 400°F.

Slice the stalks off:

4 to 6 fennel bulbs

Trim the top, thick layer of the fennel bulbs. Wash well and then quarter it lengthwise and trim out the root end. Cut each quarter into halves or thirds.

Peel:

3 large red onions

Cut the onion into wedges that are similar in size to the fennel wedges.

Combine the fennel and onions in a large bowl and coat with:

2 to 4 tbsp olive oil.

Spread the vegetables in a large roasting pan. Roast for 45 to 60 minutes, stirring every 15 minutes. The fennel should be soft through and well browned in spots.

Serve hot.

Roasted Red Pepper and Navy Bean Salad

Place on a cookie sheet under the broiler:

two red peppers

Broil until the skin turns black, rotating the red peppers to expose all sides to the heat.

Remove and cool.

Slip the black skins off the red peppers, remove the seeds, and slice into half-inch squares.

Place in a bowl with:

1 cup cooked navy beans or Great Northern beans

½ cup chopped, fresh cilantro leaves

In a small bowl combine the following and toss into the red pepper mixture:

3 tbsp almond mayonnaise   **1 small clove garlic, crushed**

1 tbsp olive oil   **black pepper to taste**

Serve at room temperature.

Note: You can use commercial soy mayonnaise if you are not intolerant to soy.

Roasted Vegetables #1

This combination has an Italian aroma because of the rosemary. Eat with a side salad which is dressed with a vinaigrette dressing.

Preheat oven to 350°F.

Place some or all of the following ingredients in a roasting pan:

- **onions, quartered**
- **beets, quartered**
- **carrots, peeled and cut into 2" pieces**
- **parsnips, peeled and cut into 2" pieces**
- **yams, peeled and cut into 1" cubes**
- **zucchini, cut into 1" slices**
- **turnips, quartered**
- **red peppers, cut into 1" strips**
- **garlic cloves, halved**

Toss with:

- **olive oil**
- **fresh or dried rosemary**
- **black pepper to taste**

Bake for 40 to 50 minutes, or until tender, stirring after 20 minutes.

Variation: Use the roasted vegetables as a topping for rice pasta instead of the traditional tomato sauce.

Roasted Vegetables #2

*This combination has an amazing effect on the senses.
It is hard to know what to concentrate on;
the spicy, the sweet, the sour, or the pungent!*

Preheat oven to 350°F.

Place the following ingredients in a 9"x13" roasting pan:

- **1 onion, halved and slice thin**
- **half a fennel (anise) bulb, cored and sliced thin**
- **5 carrots, cut into match sticks**
- **2 large parsnips, cut into match sticks**
- **1 cup fresh cranberries**

Toss with:

- **2 to 3 tbsp olive oil**
- **cayenne pepper to taste**   **black pepper to taste**

Bake for 40 to 50 minutes, or until tender, stirring after 20 minutes.

Variation: Use the roasted vegetables as a topping for rice pasta instead of the traditional tomato sauce.

Roasted Vegetables #3

Preheat oven to 425°F.

Clean and trim all of the vegetables. Cut them all into one inch cubes and place in a big bowl:

2 onions	**2 large, ripe tomatoes**
2 large fennel bulbs	**1 large red pepper**
10 small carrots	

Toss with:

3 tbsp olive oil	**2/3 cup Basil Tomato Sauce**
6 cloves garlic, minced	**black pepper to taste**

Spread onto two baking sheets and roast for 50 to 60 minutes, or until tender, stirring every 10 minutes.

Variation: Use the roasted vegetables as a topping for rice pasta instead of the traditional tomato sauce.

Scalloped Yams and Apples

Preheat oven to 350°F.

Clean, peel, and cut into ¼ inch slices:

1 ½ pounds yams

Peel, core, and cut into ¼ inch slices:

¾ pound Granny Smith apples

Arrange the yams in an oiled low-sided baking pan and insert a slice of apple between every two or three yam slices.

Drizzle on:

2 tbsp olive oil   **3 tbsp lemon juice**

Bake 40 to 50 minutes, or until the yams are tender and lightly browned.

Sesame Vegetables

Place in a dry sauté pan and roast, stirring constantly, until golden brown:

1/3 cup sesame seeds

Heat to brown spices:

2 tbsp olive oil **1 tsp ground cumin**

½ tsp ground black pepper

Add the following and sauté until slightly tender:

½ onion, sliced into thin wedges **1 stalk celery, sliced thin**

1 carrot, sliced thin **1 cup broccoli florets**

½ red pepper, sliced thin **1 cup cauliflower florets**

Add toasted sesame seeds.

Serve with peeled and boiled potatoes or yams.

Spiced Pumpkin Soup

Peel, seed and chop:

> **4 cups baking pumpkin**

Set aside.

In a large saucepan sauté until the onion is translucent, but not brown:

2 tbsp olive oil	**½ tsp ground cinnamon**
1 onion, cut into thin wedges	**½ tsp ground ginger**
½ tsp ground turmeric	**½ tsp ground coriander**
1 tsp ground cumin	

Add the pumpkin and:

> **3 carrots, peeled and chopped**   **10 cups water**

Cook until carrots and pumpkin are tender.

Purée and return to the pot.

Heat through and serve.

Tomato Zucchini Sauce

This sauce is great to use for pizza sauce, put on pasta, to make casseroles with, or to dip bread into.

In a large pot sauté the following until the onion is translucent, but not brown:

2 tbsp olive oil **2 cloves garlic, crushed**

2 onions, finely chopped

Add the grated zucchini and sauté an additional 10 minutes:

2 medium zucchini, medium grated

Add the remaining ingredients and simmer for 30 minutes:

one 28 oz can tomato purée **black pepper to taste**

20 fresh basil leaves, or 1 tbsp dried basil

Zucchini with Raisins and Pine Nuts

In a large skillet sauté onion until soft and beginning to brown:

2 tbsp olive oil   **3 ½ cups onion, in thin wedges**

Add the summer squashes and cook until barely tender, 2 to 5 minutes:

¾ pound zucchini, julienned

¾ pound yellow squash, julienned

Cook for a few minutes longer with:

2 tbsp balsamic vinegar   **¼ cup raisins**

¼ cup pine nuts   **black pepper to taste**

Serve hot or at room temperature.

SALADS

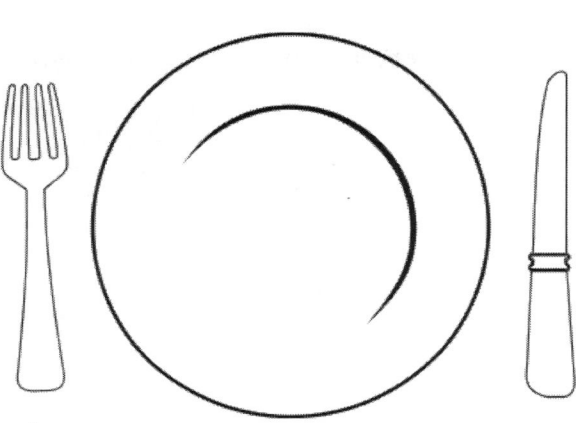

Avocado Dressing 62
Dijon Mustard Dressing... 63
French Dressing.. 64
Ginger-Sesame Dressing 65
Lime Vinaigrette 66
Sesame Salad Dressing 67
Tofu Sesame Dressing 68
Avocado Salad.. 69
Bean Sprout Salad 70
Carrot Celery Salad 71
Cooked Vegetable Salad 72
Green Bean Salad 73
Kale Salad 74
Marinated Salad.. 75
Spinach Salad 76
Tabouli.. 77
Waldorf Salad... 78
Watercress and Radicchio Salad 79

Avocado Dressing

Blend all ingredients until smooth with a fork or in an electric blender:

- ¼ cup lemon juice
- ¼ cup olive oil
- 1 large ripe avocado
- dash of ground black pepper

Dijon Mustard Dressing

Whisk thoroughly until smooth:

½ cup olive oil

3 tbsp red wine vinegar

1 tbsp Dijon mustard

1 clove garlic, crushed

French Dressing

Whisk thoroughly until smooth:

½ cup olive oil

2 tbsp apple cider vinegar

2 tbsp lemon juice

¼ tsp ground mustard seed

¼ tsp ground paprika

2 tsp tomato paste

ground pepper to taste

Ginger-Sesame Dressing

Blend all ingredients until the ginger is nearly puréed in an electric blender:

- **2 tbsp minced fresh gingerroot**
- **2 tbsp lemon juice**
- **3 tbsp orange juice**
- **3 tbsp dark sesame oil**
- **1 tsp wheat-free soy sauce**
- **2 tbsp rice vinegar**
- **2 tbsp sesame seeds**

Lime Vinaigrette

Blend all ingredients until smooth in an electric blender:

¼ cup lime juice	2 tbsp white wine vinegar
¼ cup olive oil	½ tsp ground mustard seed
1 clove garlic	ground white pepper to taste
1 tbsp fresh coriander (cilantro)	

Sesame Salad Dressing

Blend all ingredients until smooth in an electric blender:

- ¼ cup sesame seeds or 2 tbsp tahini
- ¼ cup olive oil
- ¼ clove garlic
- juice of half a lemon
- ½ cup water
- 1 tbsp fresh parsley

Tofu Sesame Dressing

In a blender combine the following and blend until smooth and creamy:

2/3 cup tofu   **½ tsp tahini**

1 tbsp grated onion **1 tbsp lemon juice**

½ cup water

Avocado Salad

Peel, seed, and cut into thin slices:

2 avocados

Arrange on a serving dish with:

½ red onion, thinly sliced   **4 tomatoes, thinly sliced**

Dress with Lime Vinaigrette and serve.

Bean Sprout Salad

Bring to a boil:

3 cups water

Add and boil for one minute:

3 cups bean sprouts

Drain and rinse with cold water to stop the cooking process.

Toss with Ginger-Sesame Dressing.

Serve.

Carrot Celery Salad

In a bowl combine:

6 carrots, peeled and grated	**2/3 cup pecan pieces**
2 stalks celery, thinly sliced	**1 cup dried currants or raisins**

Variation: Try thin pieces of fennel (anise) bulb in addition to, or instead of, celery.

Dress with:

6 tbsp olive oil	**4 tbsp rice vinegar**

Serve.

Cooked Vegetable Salad

Cut into 1" by 2" pieces:

2 cups mixture of carrots, cauliflower, and peppers

In a pot combine:

2/3 cup white vinegar   **1 cup water**

Bring to a boil and add the vegetables. When the water returns to a boil, drain and place in a serving bowl.

Dress the vegetables with a mixture of:

½ cup olive oil   **black pepper to taste**

1 tbsp finely chopped parsley or chives

1 clove garlic, crushed

Green Bean Salad

Snap off the ends and steam until tender:

    4 cups green beans.

Drain and place in a serving bowl and top with:

    ½ cup chopped fresh parsley   **3 cloves garlic, thinly sliced**

Toss with:

    ¼ cup olive oil   **3 tbsp rice vinegar**

Serve.

Kale Salad

Bring to a boil:

    ½ cup water

Add and boil until it wilts:

    one pound fresh kale, cleaned, stalks removed, and cut into ribbons

Drain.

Allow to cool.

Toss with Ginger-Sesame Dressing.

Serve.

Marinated Salad

Snap off the ends and steam for five minutes:

2 cups green beans

Add and steam an additional 5 to 7 minutes:

2 cups broccoli florets

2 cups cauliflower florets

1 cup asparagus spears, in 2 inch pieces

Drain and rinse with cold water to stop the cooking process.

Transfer to a bowl and add:

one can artichoke hearts, drained and cut into halves

1 ½ cups cooked chickpeas

1/3 cup pitted black olives, halved

1 small zucchini, thinly sliced

Toss with French Dressing and refrigerate for at least two hours.

Serve.

Spinach Salad

Combine and let sit for 10 to 30 minutes to allow flavors to blend:

2 cups baby spinach leaves   **1 apple, peeled and grated**

2 carrots, grated

Serve.

Tabouli

In a large bowl combine all ingredients.

- **1 cup cooked quinoa**
- **2 tomatoes, finely chopped**
- **1 small stalk celery, finely chopped**
- **1 small cucumber, finely chopped**
- **1 small onion, finely chopped**
- **½ red pepper, finely chopped**
- **1 bunch parsley, chopped**
- **2 tbsp olive oil**
- **juice of 2 lemons**

Store in refrigerator from one day up to two weeks.

Waldorf Salad

Combine the following ingredients and mix with the Tofu Sesame Dressing.

- **3 ½ cups shredded cabbage**
- **¼ cup celery, sliced thin**
- **¼ cup grated carrot**
- **one apple, cut into ½ inch cubes**
- **½ cup toasted walnuts**
- **¼ cup raisins**

Note: To toast the walnuts spread raw walnuts on a baking sheet and bake in a 400°F oven for 5 to 10 minutes.

Watercress and Radicchio Salad

Combine the following ingredients and toss with the Ginger-Sesame Dressing.

- **6 cups watercress leaves, loosely packed**
- **4 cups torn radicchio leaves, loosely packed**
- **2 heads Belgian endive, cut into ribbons**
- **1 fennel bulb, cored and cut into thin slices**
- one green apple, cut into ½ inch cubes
- ½ cup dried apricots, cut into thin slices

STARCHES

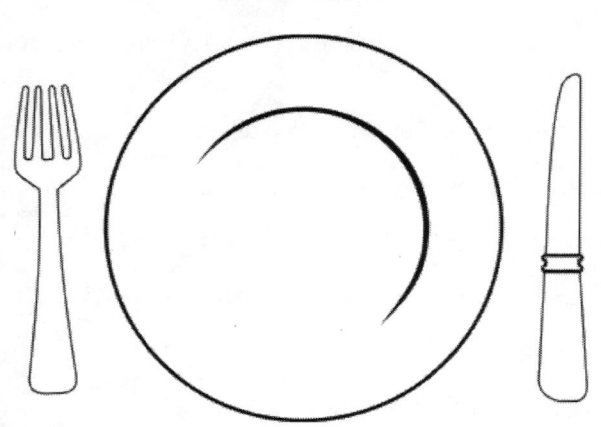

Basic Millet	81
Basic Quinoa	82
Basic Rice	83
Brown Rice Chili	84
Buckwheat Pilaf	85
Curried Oat Groats	86
Curried Rice Salad	87
Garlic Rosemary Potatoes	88
Garlic Walnut Brown Rice	89
Hash Brown Potatoes	90
High Protein Oatmeal	91
Indian Flat Bread	92
Mediterranean Pasta Salad	94
Millet Polenta	95
Millet and Squash	96
Pesto Pasta Salad	97
Quinoa Stir Fry	98
Rice Stir Fry	99
Rice Vermicelli Salad	100
Three Grain Salad	101

Basic Millet

Whenever a recipe calls for couscous use either millet or quinoa.

Bring to a boil in a covered pot.

4 cups water

Add the following, reduce heat as low as possible, cover and simmer until all the water is absorbed (15 to 20 minutes).

2 cups millet

Remove from heat and fluff with a fork.

Basic Quinoa

Whenever a recipe calls for couscous use either millet or quinoa.

Bring to a boil in a covered pot.

3 cups water

Add the following, reduce heat as low as possible, cover and simmer until all the water is absorbed (15 to 20 minutes).

2 cups quinoa

Remove from heat and fluff with a fork.

Basic Rice

The proportions are the same regardless of whether you are cooking brown rice or white rice; it is the cooking time that will change.

Bring to a boil in a covered pot.

    3 cups water

Add the following, reduce heat as low as possible, cover, and simmer until all the water is absorbed (15 to 20 minutes for white rice and 40 to 50 minutes for brown rice).

    2 cups rice

Remove from heat and fluff with a fork.

Note: You can dress up the rice by sprinkling toasted sesame seeds and thinly sliced green onions on top.

Brown Rice Chili

This recipe calls for cooked brown rice so it comes in handy when you have some left over!

In a saucepan soak overnight:

½ pound dried pinto beans

Drain and cover with fresh water. Bring to a boil, reduce heat, and simmer until beans are tender (40 to 60 minutes). Drain and set aside.

In a large pot sauté over medium heat until barely tender:

3 tbsp olive oil	**1 stalk celery, chopped**
1 onion, chopped	**2 cups green beans, ½" lengths**
1 clove garlic, crushed	**3 cups mushrooms, sliced**
1 red pepper, finely chopped	

1 or 2 small hot chili peppers, seeded and finely chopped

Add spices and brown for one minute:

½ tsp cayenne pepper	**2 tbsp chili powder**
1 tbsp paprika	**½ tsp ground black pepper**
1 tsp ground cumin	

Reduce heat and add:

one 28 ounce can tomato purée	**cooked beans**

Simmer for 30 minutes.

Add:

1 ½ cups cooked brown rice	**1 ½ cups water**
¼ cup fresh cilantro, chopped	

Cook until heated through, 10 to 15 minutes. Serve.

Buckwheat Pilaf

In a heavy saucepan heat over low heat for five minutes:

1 ½ cups buckwheat groats (raw, not toasted)

1 tbsp olive oil

Add the following, reduce heat as low as possible, cover, and simmer until all the water is absorbed and buckwheat is tender:

1 onion, diced

3 medium potatoes, peeled and cut into ¼ inch cubes

3 stalks celery, cut into ¼ inch cubes

2 ½ cups boiling water

½ tsp dried thyme

3 tbsp wheat-free soy sauce

Season with:

ground black pepper to taste

Garnish with:

minced chives or green onions to taste

Serve.

Curried Oat Groats

In a saucepan bring to a boil:

> **1 ¾ cups water**

Add:

> **1 cup oat groats** **¼ cup sesame seeds**
>
> **½ cup raisins** **2 tsp curry powder**
>
> **¼ cup shredded coconut**

Cover, reduce heat, and simmer until the water is absorbed, approximately 30 minutes.

Toast in a 350°F oven for 5 to 10 minutes:

> **¼ cup slivered almonds**

Sprinkle almonds over oat groats and serve with a side salad.

Curried Rice Salad

Soak for one hour then drain and set aside:

    ½ cup raisins   warm water to cover

Prepare according to Basic Rice recipe:

    2 cups brown basmati rice   **3 tbsp curry powder**

    3 cups water

Rinse and drain cooked rice in cold water.

Transfer to a large serving bowl and add:

    1 ½ cups hazelnuts   drained raisins

    1 large can small peas, drained (or 1 ½ cups cooked peas)

Dress with:

    1 cup mayonnaise   **½ cup lemon juice**

    (Almond Mayonnaise or store-bought soy mayonnaise)

Season with:

    ground black pepper to taste

Refrigerate for at least two hours before serving.

Garlic Rosemary Potatoes

These quantities are per person.

In a nonstick pan sauté over medium heat until tender (30 to 40 minutes:

2 medium potatoes, peeled and cut into one inch cubes

1 clove garlic, minced **ground black pepper to taste**

1 tsp fresh rosemary, chopped **2 tbsp olive oil**

Stir enough that the potatoes do not burn, but not so much that they break apart.

Note: You can bake these potatoes in a 350°F oven for 35 to 45 minutes, stirring once after 25 minutes.

Variation: Add one turnip, peeled and cubed.

Garlic Walnut Brown Rice

Pour into a saucepan and bring to a boil:

3 cups water

Add:

juice of half a lemon   **2 cups raw brown rice**

Cover, reduce heat, and simmer until the water is absorbed (30 to 40 minutes).

Pound together the following until a smooth paste is formed:

3 tbsp chopped parsley   **2 cloves garlic**

¼ cup walnuts

Gradually beat in:

3 tbsp olive oil

Season to taste with:

black pepper

Blend in the nut mixture into the rice and serve.

Hash Brown Potatoes

Note: This recipe gives the quantities per person.

Use a coarse grater to grate:

    1 medium potato, peeled

Place in a heated sauté pan with:

    2 tbsp olive oil   **½ clove garlic, finely chopped**

    ¼ medium onion, finely chopped

Cook until potatoes are brown and tender.

Season with:

    freshly ground black pepper, to taste

Serve.

Variation: Add ½ grated turnip per person.

High Protein Oatmeal

Preheat oven to 400°F.

Bake on a cookie sheet until golden (about 5 to 8 minutes):

1 cup thick rolled oats

Remove from oven and place in a saucepan with:

5 cups white grape juice   **¼ cup cashew butter**

Heat until it boils. Reduce heat and simmer for 20 minutes.

Mix in:

1 tsp ground cinnamon   **1 tsp vanilla extract**

Serve.

Indian Flat Bread

These flat breads are called dosas which are like French crêpes or Mexican tortillas. They require a lot of time and patience but are worth it!

The ingredients for these dosas are:

½ cup urad dal	**1 cup basmati rice**
water	

Pick over the urad dal (a kind of lentil which is available at Indian food stores) and discard any discolored lentils. Wash several times in water until the water is clear. Place in a bowl with 3 cups water to let soak.

Wash the rice until the rinse water is clear. Place in a bowl, separate from the dal, with 3 cups of water to let soak.

Soak the rice and the dal for 10 to 12 hours.

Drain the dal and place in a blender with enough fresh water to just cover. Blend at high speed until the mixture becomes like a thick batter. Put into a bowl.

Drain the rice and place in the blender with enough water to just cover. Blend at high speed until the mixture becomes like a thick batter. Put into the bowl with the ground dal and cover tightly with plastic wrap.

Let the ground dal and rice mixture ferment at room temperature for 12 hours.

Cook the dosas in a greased heavy 8 to 12 inch sauté pan over medium heat. Pour in ½ cup batter (you may have to add some water to get the right consistency) and tip the pan from side to side to spread the batter evenly into a flat bread.

Cook for 2 to 3 minutes, until the dosa starts to detach from the pan. Turn the dosa over and cook an additional 2 to 3 minutes. Transfer to a heated serving plate, and drape a kitchen towel over it to keep it warm.

Grease the pan and cook the next dosa.

Serve the dosas warm or at room temperature with curried chickpeas or vegetable chili.

Mediterranean Pasta Salad

Cook as per directions on pasta package:

3 cups uncooked rice pasta (shells, spirals, or elbows)

Drain and rinse with cold water. Set aside.

Mix together the following ingredients and add the cooked pasta:

- **1 cup diced red pepper**
- **½ cup black olives, sliced**
- **1 ½ cups canned artichokes, drained and cut into thirds**
- **2 carrots, peeled and grated**
- **2 cups cherry tomatoes**

Toss with the dressing below and refrigerate 2 to 4 hours.

- **1/3 cup lemon juice**
- **2 tbsp green onions, sliced thin**
- **1 tbsp fresh oregano, or 1 tsp dried oregano**
- **¼ cup olive oil**
- **1 clove garlic, minced**

Serve on lettuce leaves.

Millet Polenta

These slabs of millet polenta are wonderful served with flavorful bean dishes or sauces on top.

In a one quart oven proof casserole (preferably square) bring to a boil:

3 cups water

Add:

1 cup millet

Reduce heat and simmer, covered, 20 minutes or until seeds start to open.

Preheat oven to 350°F.

Cover the casserole dish and place in the oven. Bake for 30 to 40 minutes, or until the millet is slightly crusted and firm to the touch.

Remove from oven, cool, and then refrigerate.

When you are ready to use it, slice into ¾ inch to 1 inch slabs. Sauté in olive oil until heated through and golden.

Millet and Squash

In a heavy pot sauté until translucent:

2 small or one medium onion, sliced   2 tbsp olive oil

Add:

1 cup chopped celery   **1 tsp ground cinnamon**

½ tsp ground allspice   **3 ½ cups water**

2 cups millet, rinsed and drained

2 cups peeled and diced butternut squash

Bring to a boil. Cover and reduce heat to minimum. Simmer until the liquid is absorbed and the millet is tender.

Pesto Pasta Salad

Cook as per directions on pasta package:

2 cups uncooked rice pasta (shells, spirals, or elbows)

Drain and rinse with cold water. Set aside.

Mix together the following ingredients and add the cooked pasta:

½ cup red pepper, finely diced

½ cup celery, finely sliced

½ cup cucumber, cut into small cubes

Toss with:

3 tbsp pesto

Refrigerate at least an hour.

Serve with green bean salad.

Quinoa Stir Fry

Prepare and set aside:

2 cups cooked quinoa (see basic quinoa recipe)

Stir fry over high heat until vegetables are barely tender:

1 cup mushrooms, sliced	**1 cup broccoli florets**
½ cup celery, sliced	**1 clove garlic, crushed**
½ cup carrot, sliced	**2 to 4 tbsp olive oil**
1 onion, sliced	

Stir in and then heat through:

cooked quinoa	**1 cup bean sprouts**
½ cup sliced almonds	**wheat-free soy sauce, to taste**

Serve immediately.

Rice Stir Fry

Cook and set aside:

2 cups rice (about 4 cups cooked, see basic rice recipe)

Stir fry over high heat for two minute:

3 tbsp sesame oil	**1 clove garlic, finely chopped**
2/3 cup chopped green onions	**2 tbsp grated fresh ginger**
4 stalks celery, thinly sliced	

Add and cook an additional minute:

½ cup sliced water chestnuts	**2 cups bean sprouts**
½ cup sunflower seeds	

Add the rice and cook until heated through.

Season with:

wheat-free soy sauce, to taste

Serve immediately.

Rice Vermicelli Salad

Cook in ample water for two minutes, or until soft:

>½ **pound rice vermicelli**

Strain and rinse with cold water.

Cook in ample water for one minute:

>½ **pound pea pods (snow peas), cleaned with ends snapped off**

Strain and rinse with cold water to stop the cooking process.

Combine the rice vermicelli and pea pods with:

½ **pound mushrooms, thinly sliced**	**2 tbsp olive oil**
1 red pepper, thinly sliced	**2 tsp sesame oil**
¼ **cup sesame seeds**	**1 tbsp minced fresh gingerroot**
2/3 cup sliced water chestnuts	**2 large cloves garlic, minced**
6 tbsp wheat-free soy sauce	**1 tbsp rice vinegar**

Marinate noodles for one hour before serving.

Three Grain Salad

In a saucepan toast for three minutes:

    1 tbsp olive oil   **1 cup brown rice**

    1 bay leaf   **1 cup whole grain barley**

Add:

    3 ½ cups water

Bring to a boil then reduce heat, cover, and simmer until grains are soft (40 to 50 minutes).

Drain off excess water and spread grains on a baking sheet to cool.

In a bowl combine and let sit for 15 minutes:

    2/3 cup boiling water   **2/3 cup quinoa**

Fluff the quinoa and spread on a baking sheet to cool.

Once the grains are cool combine them in a serving bowl and toss with:

    2/3 cup olive oil   **1/3 cup chopped parsley**

    ½ cup wine vinegar   **2 cloves garlic, minced**

    2/3 cup chopped red onion   **ground black pepper to taste**

    ¼ cup green onions, thinly sliced

Serve cold or at room temperature.

LEGUMES

Note that canned beans are called for in the recipes
but you can use freshly cooked beans.
Soak beans overnight. Replace water. Cook until done.
Put in containers, cover with fresh water, and freeze for later use.

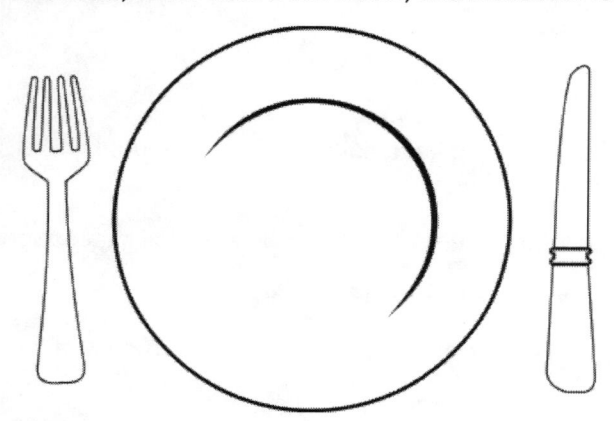

Azuki Bean Soup 103
Bean Salad I 104
Bean Salad II 105
Chickpea Dip 106
Chickpea and Spinach Soup 107
Curried Chickpeas 108
Falafel with Tahini Sauce 109
Lima Beans Salad 110
Lima Beans in Tomato Sauce 111
Mixed Bean Soup 112
Navy Beans Provençale 113
Sesame Crusted Tofu 114
Soy Yogurt 115
Tofu Quiche 116
Tuscan Kidney Beans With Sage 117
Vegetable Chili 118

Azuki Bean Soup

Wash:

    1 ½ cups azuki beans

Add and cook until beans are almost done:

    10 cups water

Drain the beans.

Sauté in a soup pot until golden brown:

    2 tbsp olive oil　　　　　　　　**1 onion, diced**

    1 ½ cups diced butternut squash

Add and cook until everything is tender:

    cooked azuki beans　　　　　　**5 cups fresh water**

Add:

    wheat-free soy sauce or wheat-free tamari, to taste

Garnish with:

    green onion slices or chopped fresh parsley

Serve.

Bean Salad I

Stem until just tender:

    1 cup green beans　　　　　　**1 cup yellow beans**

Drain and cool.

Add:

    one 15 ounce can chickpeas (rinsed and drained)

    one 15 ounce can red kidney beans (rinsed and drained)

    one 15 ounce can white kidney beans (rinsed and drained)

    ½ cup thinly sliced red onion

Marinate, for 3 to 4 hours before serving, in:

    1/3 cup olive oil　　　　　　**½ tsp dried oregano**

    1/3 cup white wine vinegar

Bean Salad II

Combine the following ingredients in a bowl:

- **one 15 ounce can of chickpeas (rinsed and drained)**
- **one 15 ounce can of black-eyed peas (rinsed and drained)**
- **one 15 ounce can of red kidney beans (rinsed and drained)**
- **one red pepper, seeded and cubed**
- **5 green onions, finely chopped**

Whisk together:

- **2 tbsp olive oil**
- **1/3 cup lemon juice**
- **1/8 tsp ground black pepper**
- **pinch of cayenne pepper**
- **1/3 cup chopped fresh cilantro (coriander)**

Pour the dressing over the bean mixture and toss gently. Marinate 4 to 6 hours minimum before serving.

Chickpea Dip

Blend together all the ingredients in a food processor or blender:

2 cups drained cooked chickpeas

1 clove crushed garlic

2 tbsp tahini

½ cup olive oil

¼ cup water

juice of half a lemon

1 tbsp chopped, fresh chives or parsley

If you prefer a thinner consistency add a few tablespoons of water.

Serve with raw vegetable sticks for dipping.

Chickpea and Spinach Soup

In a heavy saucepan cook until soft:

- **1 tbsp olive oil**
- **4 cloves garlic, minced**
- **2 medium onions, chopped**

Add and cook for one minute:

- **1 potato, peeled and cut into one inch cubes**

Add the following ingredients then cover and simmer until the potato is tender, about 15 minutes:

- **4 cups water**
- **2 tbsp chopped fresh parsley**
- **2 tbsp chopped fresh coriander (cilantro)**
- **1 tsp dried marjoram**

Stir in:

- **2 cups cooked chickpeas**

Purée the soup and return to the pot.

Add and simmer for five minutes.

- **10 ounces fresh spinach, trimmed and chopped**

Serve.

Curried Chickpeas

In a saucepan heat the following together until the seeds start to pop:

- **3 tbsp olive oil**
- **½ tsp cumin seeds**
- **½ tsp black mustard seeds**

Add and cook until onions are translucent, but not brown:

- **1 onion, finely chopped**
- **2 stalks celery, finely chopped**

Add spices and cook for a minute for the flavors to set:

- **½ tsp turmeric**
- **½ tsp ground cumin**
- **½ tsp ground coriander**
- **½ tsp curry powder**
- **½ tsp ground ginger**
- **dash of cayenne pepper**

Add:

- **2 cans chickpeas (garbanzos) drained and rinsed**
- **water to just cover chickpeas**

Cover and simmer over low heat for approximately 45 minutes.

Falafel with Tahini Sauce

Soak overnight:

> **2 cups chickpeas**   **water**

Drain and process until smooth in a food processor with:

> **1 large onion, quartered**   **1 tbsp ground cumin**
>
> **½ cup minced parsley**   **1 tbsp ground coriander**
>
> **2 cloves garlic, crushed**
>
> **1 tsp black pepper or ¼ tsp cayenne pepper**

Let mixture stand for a minimum of one hour to a maximum of 3 days to allow flavors to blend.

When you are ready to cook the falafel shape the mixture into small balls or patties, about one inch in diameter. Sauté in a large saucepan until balls or patties are crisp in:

> **olive oil to cover the bottom of the pan**

Serve warm with a tahini sauce made by blending together:

> **¼ cup tofu**   **¼ cup tahini**
>
> **2 tbsp lemon juice**   **4 tbsp hot water**

Note: If you like the tahini sauce thinner add additional hot water.

Lima Beans Salad

Soak overnight then cook in fresh water until barely tender:

    1 ½ cups large lima beans   **water**

Drain and cool.

Once the lima beans are cool combine with:

2 large tomatoes, cut into wedges	**3 tbsp red wine vinegar**
¼ cup chopped fresh parsley	**¼ cup olive oil**
8 green onions, thinly sliced	**¼ tsp dried oregano**
1 clove garlic, crushed	**ground black pepper to taste**

Allow the salad to sit and marinate for a minimum of 2 hours before serving for best results.

Lima Beans in Tomato Sauce

Soak overnight then cook in fresh water until barely tender:

    1 ½ cups large lima beans　　　　**water**

Drain and set aside.

Sauté in a large saucepan until onion is translucent but not brown:

    2 to 3 onions, cut into thin wedges

    6 to 10 whole cloves of garlic　　　　**¼ cup olive oil**

Add:

    cooked lima beans

    1 ½ cups tomato sauce, tomato purée or canned whole tomatoes

Season to taste with:

    ground black pepper　　　　**cayenne pepper**

Serve warm or at room temperature.

Mixed Bean Soup

Wash and place in a saucepan:

    ½ cup lentils   **¼ cup white navy beans**

    ¼ cup yellow split peas   **1 cup azuki beans**

Add and bring to a boil:

    7 cups water

Turn off heat and let beans sit for thirty minutes. Drain the beans and set aside.

Sauté in the saucepan until golden brown:

    2 tbsp olive oil

    ½ onion, diced   **1 stalk celery, finely diced**

Add and cook until everything is tender, 30 to 45 minutes:

    2 tsp dried basil   **2 tsp dried thyme**

    1 tsp ground black pepper   **1 tsp ground cumin**

    1 bay leaf   **cooked beans**

    8 cups fresh water

Garnish with:

    sliced green onions

Serve.

Navy Beans Provençale

Soak overnight then cook in fresh water until barely tender:

    1 ¼ cups navy beans   **water**

Drain and set aside.

Pour boiling water over:

    1 large tomato   **water**

When the skin cracks pour off the water and peel the tomato. Cut in half and push out the seeds. Coarsely chop and set aside.

Sauté in a large saucepan until onion is translucent but not brown:

    ¼ cup olive oil   **2 onions, cut into thin wedges**

    2 cloves of garlic, sliced   **dash of cayenne pepper**

Toss with:

    cooked navy beans   **chopped tomato**

    ¼ cup of chopped fresh parsley   **1 tbsp fresh dried thyme**

    1 tbsp fresh dried sage   **1 tbsp fresh dried rosemary**

    1 bay leaf

Pour into an oiled casserole dish and barely cover with:

    Fresh water

Cover and bake for 1 ½ hours at 350°F.

Serve (perhaps with baked yams and steamed broccoli).

Note: If you do not have fresh herbs use 1 tsp of dried herbs for each tablespoon called for.

Sesame Crusted Tofu

This recipe does not recommend specific amounts of ingredients. Use your imagination and your own ingredient proportions to make your own masterpiece.

Cut half-inch slices of tofu and closely pack them in a shallow roasting pan.

tofu

Combine:

sesame seeds (natural, hulled, black, or a combination)

crushed garlic **hot chili paste**

wheat-free soy sauce **green onions (finely sliced)**

Spoon sesame seed mixture over the tofu and let marinate one hour.

Bake for 40 to 60 minutes at 350°F.

Serve hot or at room temperature.

Soy Yogurt

The only dairy-free milk that works to make yogurt is soymilk. Please make sure that you are not intolerant to soy before you ingest large quantities of it.

Heat unsweetened soy milk until it feels just warm when you put your finger in it.

Mix with a yogurt starter and pour into covered glass jars (or into the containers in a yogurt maker). Note: You can purchase the yogurt starter at a health food store.

Place in the oven, with the oven light on for warmth (or the pilot light if you have a gas oven), and leave 8 to 9 hours.

Remove and refrigerate.

Note: Once you have made a batch of yogurt, keep ½ cup aside to use instead of the starter for each new quart batch that you are going to make.

Tofu Quiche

Preheat oven to 350°F.

For the quiche crust, combine until you form a dough that is easy to handle:

- **1/3 cup olive oil**
- **1 tbsp flaxseed "goop"**
- **1 ½ cups barley flour**
- **1 to 2 tbsp water**

Press into a quiche pan or into a pie plate. Set aside.

In a sauté pan cook over medium-high heat until barely tender:

- **2 tbsp olive oil**
- **1 clove garlic, crushed**
- **1 small zucchini, finely chopped**
- **1 onion, finely chopped**
- **½ red pepper, finely chopped**

Add and cook until wilted:

- **1 cup spinach leaves, chopped**

Remove from heat and set aside.

In a blender or food processor combine:

- **2 cups soft tofu**
- **2 tsp vinegar**
- **1 clove garlic, crushed**
- **½ tsp ground black pepper**
- **1 tbsp lemon juice**
- **1 tbsp olive oil**
- **1 tsp dried basil**

Mix tofu mixture with the cooked vegetables and pour into the crust.

Bake until filling is set, about 30 to 40 minutes.

Serve warm.

Variation: Make crust with millet by cooking ½ cup millet in 1 ½ cups water until a porridge is formed. Spread into a greased quiche dish or pie plate and allow to cool. Pour in above filling and bake.

Tuscan Kidney Beans With Sage

In a large saucepan over medium heat cook until liquid is absorbed, about 20 minutes:

    2 large tomatoes, coarsely chopped

    1 tbsp fresh sage, chopped   **1 clove garlic, minced**

Add and cook until heated through:

    3 cups cooked kidney beans

Remove from heat and stir in:

    1 tbsp olive oil   **1 tbsp red wine vinegar**

    ground black pepper to taste

Serve.

Vegetable Chili

Sauté until onion is golden but not brown:

>**1 onion, chopped** **2 to 3 tbsp olive oil**

Mix in and brown:

>**1 tbsp chili powder** **1 tsp cumin powder**

Add and cook until summer squash is tender:

>**One 28 ounce can of ground tomatoes**
>
>**½ cup water**
>
>**1 red pepper, chopped**
>
>**2 medium green zucchini, cubed**
>
>**2 medium yellow summer squash, cubed**
>
>**three 15 ounce cans of beans, rinsed and drained**

(chickpeas, kidney beans, black-eyed peas, great northern beans, etc.)

Serve warm or at room temperature with wheat-free bread and a side salad.

DESSERTS

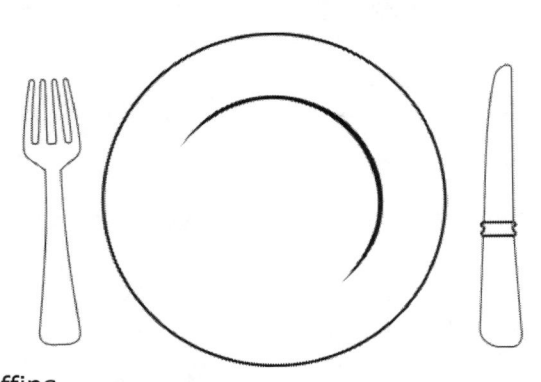

Amaranth Muffins	120
Apple Flax Treat	121
Apple Oat Dessert	122
Arrowroot Pancakes	123
Barley Pancakes	124
Blueberry Crisp	125
Brown Rice Pudding	126
Buckwheat Currant Dessert	127
Chocolate Pudding	128
Cranberry Muffins	129
Energy Balls	130
Fruit in "Gelatin"	131
Fruit Juice Muffins	132
Granola	133
Indian Fruit Bake	134
Indian Pudding	135
Nut-Apricot Cobbler	136
Nut-Carob Cookies	137
Nut Pancakes	138
Oatmeal and Fruit Pudding	139
Peach Crisp	140
Pear Crumble	141
Poached Peaches	142
Raisin Pudding	143
Raisin-Sauced Pears	144
Rice Flour Pancakes	145
Strawberries and Lemon	146
Tapioca Pudding I	147
Tapioca Pudding II	148

Amaranth Muffins

Preheat oven to 350°F.

Combine the following ingredients in a bowl:

    1 ¾ cups amaranth flour   **¼ cup tapioca starch**

    1 tsp cinnamon   ,   **½ tsp baking powder**

In another bowl mix together:

    ½ tsp vanilla extract   **¼ cup olive oil**

    3/4 cup pineapple juice   **4 tbsp date spread**

Combine the wet and dry ingredients and spoon into greased or lined muffin tins.

Bake for 20 minutes, or until an inserted toothpick comes out clean.

Variations: Add1 cup chopped dates or 1 cup blueberries, or ¼ copped hazelnuts to batter.

Apple Flax Treat

The quantities here are per person.

Combine:

2 apples, grated   **2 tbsp ground flaxseeds**

¼ cup chopped walnuts

Serve immediately for breakfast or a snack.

Apple Oat Dessert

The quantities here are per person.

Soak for 2 hours:

    1 tbsp rolled oats or barley flakes   **3 tbsp water**

Add:

    2 medium apples, peeled and grated

    1 tbsp lemon juice

Sprinkle with:

    1 tbsp ground almonds or hazelnuts

    1 tsp ground flaxseeds

Serve immediately.

Arrowroot Pancakes

Process in a food processor or blender until uniform in consistency:

1 cup sesame seeds   **½ cup arrowroot starch**

2 tsp baking powder   **1 tsp guar gum**

Transfer to a bowl and add:

1 cup pineapple juice   **2 tbsp olive oil**

Mix together and add water if the batter is too thick

Pour spoonfuls onto a hot griddle and turn when the batter bubbles. Serve when done.

Note: You can use tapioca starch instead or arrowroot starch.

Barley Pancakes

Mix together:

1 ¼ cups barley flakes **½ cup tapioca starch**

1 tsp baking powder **1 tsp guar gum**

In another bowl mix together:

2 ½ cups water **2 tbsp olive oil**

3 tbsp date spread **½ tsp vanilla extract**

Mix the wet ingredients into the dry ingredients. Let the mixture sit for five to ten minutes. If the batter becomes too thick add some more water.

Pour spoonfuls onto a hot griddle, turn when the batter bubbles, then remove.

Blueberry Crisp

Preheat oven to 400°F.

Place in a greased casserole dish:

> **2 cups fresh or frozen blueberries**

Grind in a blender or food processor:

> **2/3 cup hazelnuts**   **¼ cup sesame seeds**

Moisten nut and seed mixture with:

> **2 tbsp apple juice**

Spread nut mixture over the blueberries.

Bake for about 15 minutes.

Serve warm or at room temperature.

Brown Rice Pudding

Preheat oven to 325°F.

Mix together and place in a greased casserole dish:

2 cups cooked short grain brown rice

2 cups almond milk **½ cup date spread**

Bake 20 minutes.

Serve warm or at room temperature.

Buckwheat Currant Dessert

Preheat oven to 400°F.

Mix together:

    1 ½ cups pineapple juice　　**½ cup olive oil**

Combine and add to the wet ingredients:

    1 cup currants　　**1 cup light buckwheat flour**

    1 tsp baking soda　　**2 tsp cinnamon**

    ¼ tsp ground cloves　　**½ cup chopped hazelnuts**

    1 cup arrowroot starch (or tapioca starch)

Pour into a greased 8"x8" pan and bake for 20 to 30 minutes.

Serve warm.

Chocolate Pudding

In a blender or food processor blend until smooth:

- **1 pound tofu**
- **1 ½ cups date syrup**
- **1 ½ tsp vanilla extract**
- **¼ cup olive oil**
- **½ cup cocoa powder**

Pour into individual serving bowls and refrigerate at least three hours before serving.

Cranberry Muffins

Preheat oven to 350°F.

Combine the following ingredients in a bowl:

- **2 ½ cups oat flour**
- **1 cup oatmeal**
- **½ tsp baking soda**
- **½ tsp baking powder**

In another bowl mix together:

- **3 tbsp flaxseed "goop"**
- **½ cup olive oil**
- **2 cups applesauce**

Combine the wet and dry ingredients and fold in:

- **¾ cup fresh cranberries**

Fill muffin tins and bake for 35 to 45 minutes, or until an inserted toothpick comes out clean.

Energy Balls

Combine:

    1/3 cup date syrup　　　　　　**1/3 cup almond butter**

Mix in:

    1/3 cup sesame seeds　　　　　**2/3 cup shredded coconut**

Add to make the mixture conducive to making balls:

    puffed millet

Wet your hands and roll the mixture into balls and roll in sesame seeds to coat. Store in the refrigerator.

Note: Try replacing some of the sesame seeds with flax seeds.

Note: Try adding 2 tbsp carob powder for a change.

Fruit in "Gelatin"

Combine in a saucepan and allow to sit at room temperature for ten minutes:

> **4 cups apple juice**   **4 tbsp agar-agar flakes**
>
> **½ tsp ground nutmeg or ground mace**

Bring the mixture to a boil then reduce heat and simmer until all of the agar-agar has dissolved.

In a small bowl dissolve together:

> **2 tsp kuzu starch, or 4 tsp arrowroot starch**
>
> **4 tsp water**

Add the dissolved starch to the simmering juice mixture, stirring constantly, and cook for an additional minute or two.

Pour juice mixture into a shallow dish and cool 15 minutes or until slightly thickened. Stir in:

> **1 ½ cups sliced fruit**

Refrigerate at least an hour until juice is set.

Serve.

Fruit Juice Muffins

Preheat oven to 350°F.

Combine the following ingredients in a bowl:

- **1 ½ cups apple juice**
- **¼ cup olive oil**
- **1 tbsp flaxseed "goop"**

In another bowl mix together:

- **1 ½ cups oat flour**
- **½ tsp cinnamon**
- **2 tsp baking powder**
- **1 cup chopped almonds**

Combine the wet and dry ingredients and spoon into greased or lined muffin tins.

Bake for 20 to 25 minutes.

Granola

Preheat oven to 350°F.

In a large bowl combine:

- **2 cups rolled oats**
- **¾ cup oat flour or barley flour**
- **2/3 cup sesame seeds**
- **2/3 cup olive oil**
- **½ cup washed and drained quinoa**
- **¾ cup apple juice concentrate (half a can of frozen concentrate)**
- **2 cups barley flakes**
- **1 cup flaxseeds**
- **1 cup sliced almonds**

Spread onto two cookie sheets.

Bake for 30 minutes, mixing once after 20 minutes.

Remove from oven and mix in:

- **1 cup currants**

Cool and store in an air-tight container.

Serve with applesauce, grated apple, or soy yogurt.

Indian Fruit Bake

Preheat oven to 325°F.

In a greased two quart casserole dish combine:

4 apples, cubed	**4 pears, cut into eighths**
1 cup dried apricot halves	**¼ cup apple juice**
1 cup pecan halves	**1 tsp curry powder**

Bake for 30 to 40 minutes, mixing twice during this time.

Serve warm as a dessert or to accompany the Garlic Walnut Brown Rice.

Indian Pudding

Preheat oven to 325°F.

In a saucepan bring to a boil, reduce heat, and then simmer for five minutes:

2 ½ cups almond milk

½ cup millet (rinsed and drained)

Stir the following into the millet mixture:

1/3 cup date spread	**¼ tsp ground ginger**
¼ tsp ground nutmeg	**½ tsp cinnamon**
¼ tsp ground coriander	**2 tbsp tapioca starch**
½ cup raisins	**3 apples, peeled and chopped**

Pour into a greased 1 ½ quart casserole dish and bake for 50 minutes to one hour.

Serve warm, dusted with cinnamon.

Nut-Apricot Cobbler

Soak until soft then purée in blender until smooth:

dried, unsulfured apricots

Serve in small bowls sprinkled with:

finely chopped almonds or brazilnuts

Nut-Carob Cookies

Preheat oven to 350°F.

In a bowl mix together:

- **2 cups coconut, shredded**
- **¼ cup roasted carob powder**
- **1 cup currants**
- **1 cup chick pea flour**
- **1 cup almonds**

In another bowl beat together:

- **2 tbsp oil**
- **1 tbsp flaxseed "goop"**
- **¼ cup fruit juice**

Mix together the dry and wet ingredients.

Flatten balls of dough on an oiled cookie sheet and bake for 20 to 25 minutes.

Nut Pancakes

Mix together:

1 cup ground almonds or ground hazelnuts

½ cup tapioca starch **2 tsp baking powder**

½ tsp guar gum

In another bowl mix together:

1 cup water **2 tbsp olive oil**

2 tbsp date spread

Mix the wet ingredients into the dry ingredients.

Pour spoonfuls onto a hot griddle, turn when the batter dries, then remove.

Oatmeal and Fruit Pudding

Preheat oven to 375°F.

Combine and pour into a well-oiled casserole dish:

- **2 cups cooked oatmeal**
- **¼ cup currants**
- **2 tbsp flaxseeds**
- **1/3 cup apple juice**
- **½ cup chopped dried apple**
- **¼ cup chopped almonds**
- **1 cup diced apples or pears**

Bake for 15 to 20 minutes, or until hot. Serve immediately.

Peach Crisp

Preheat oven to 325°F.

Mix together the following ingredients and place in a 9"x13" roasting pan:

2 pounds peaches - skinned and sliced

½ cup fresh or frozen raspberries, cherries, or cranberries

3 tbsp tapioca starch

To make the topping place the following in a food processor or blender and blend until smooth:

1 cup oat flour   **½ cup dried currants**

Add the following and then place on top of the peach mixture:

2 to 3 tbsp olive oil   **1 ½ cups oats**

½ cup sliced almonds   **1 tsp almond extract**

¾ cup apple juice concentrate

Bake covered for approximately one hour or until peaches are soft when tested with a knife.

Pear Crumble

Preheat oven to 350°F.

Arrange in an 8"x8" pan:

2 pounds pears - skinned and thinly sliced

Combine and pour over the pears:

1 cup pineapple juice   **1 tsp vanilla extract**

2 tbsp tapioca starch

Combine the following and sprinkle over the pear mixture:

½ cup sliced almonds   **1 tbsp olive oil**

Bake covered for 30 to 40 minutes or until pears are soft when tested with a knife.

Poached Peaches

Place ingredients in a soup pot and bring to a boil:

- **6 cups white grape juice**
- **1 orange, thinly sliced**
- **2 whole cloves**
- **1 lemon, thinly sliced**
- **1 cinnamon stick**
- **½ tsp vanilla extract**

Add peaches, reduce heat, and simmer until peaches are tender:

- **4 to 5 whole peaches, washed**

Remove peaches. Refrigerate peaches and poaching liquid separately.

To serve spoon some poaching liquid into a shallow bowl and place a peach in it.

Serve warm or cold.

Raisin Pudding

Soak until raisins are softened:

1 cup raisins   **1 cup hot water**

Add the following and blend until smooth:

1/3 cup walnuts or pecans

Eat as is or use as a spread on crackers or to accompany a curry dish.

Raisin-Sauced Pears

Preheat oven to 350°F.

Over medium high heat cook the following combination until the mixture starts to thicken:

¼ cup raisins

½ cup white grape juice

juice of 2 oranges

1 tbsp tapioca starch

¼ tsp dry mustard

1/8 tsp ground cloves

Place, cut-side up, in a baking dish:

3 pears, halved and cored

Pour thickened liquid evenly over the pears. Sprinkle with:

¼ cup slivered almonds

Bake 20 to 30 minutes or until pears are tender.

Rice Flour Pancakes

Mix together:

    1 ¼ cups brown rice flour   ½ cup tapioca starch

    1 tsp baking powder   1 tsp guar gum

In another bowl mix together:

    2 cups water   2 tbsp olive oil

    ½ tsp vanilla extract

Mix the wet ingredients into the dry ingredients. Let sit for two minutes. If the batter becomes too thick add some more water.

Pour spoonfuls onto a hot griddle, turn when the batter bubbles, then remove.

Note: The pancakes will not brown without sweetener. If you want browned pancakes replace the water with fruit juice.

Variation: Add blueberries.

Variation: Add a mashed banana and reduce the liquid from 2 cups to 1 ½ cups.

Strawberries and Lemon

This is how my grandmother would serve fresh strawberries.

Wash, trim off greens, and cut into quarters:

    1 quart fresh strawberries

Place in a bowl and add:

    2 tbsp lemon juice

Stir to coat and let sit at room temperature for an hour before serving.

Tapioca Pudding I

Soak for 15 minutes:

2 cups almond milk   **4 tbsp quick-cooking tapioca**

Heat the mixture to the boiling point. Reduce heat and simmer, stirring occasionally, until mixture begins to thicken. Remove from heat and add:

½ tsp vanilla extract

Pour into a bowl or individual serving dishes and refrigerate.

Variation: Use fruit juice instead of almond milk.

Tapioca Pudding II

Soak for 15 minutes:

2 cups canned fruit with the juice (packed in juice)

4 tbsp quick-cooking tapioca

Heat the mixture to the boiling point. Reduce heat and simmer, stirring occasionally, until mixture begins to thicken. Remove from heat and add:

½ tsp ground cinnamon

Pour into a bowl or individual serving dishes and refrigerate.